SPOTLIGHT ON
AN EQUITABLE WORLD

VALUING DIFFERENCES

Mary Ratzer

ROSEN
PUBLISHING

Published in 2025 by The Rosen Publishing Group, Inc.
2544 Clinton Street, Buffalo, NY 14224

First Edition

Editor: Greg Roza
Book Design: Michael Flynn

Photo Credits: Cover SeventyFour/Shutterstock.com; cover, p. 3 (hands) Dedraw Studio/Shutterstock.com; (series Earth icon) v4ndhira/Shutterstock.com; p. 5 wavebreakmedia/Shutterstock.com; p. 6 CarlosBarquero/Shutterstock.com; p. 7 marekuliasz/Shutterstock.com; p. 9 Dan Rentea/Shutterstock.com; p. 10 Fabrik Bilder/Shutterstock.com; p. 11 SeventyFour/Shutterstock.com; p. 13 dboystudio/Shutterstock.com; p. 14 Sundry Photography/Shutterstock.com; p. 15 Christian Carollo/Shutterstock.com; p. 16 Silent O/Shutterstock.com; p. 17 Mahmoud Suhail/Shutterstock.com; p. 19 Sean P. Aune/Shutterstock.com; p. 21 CarlosBarquero/Shutterstock.com; p. 22 Iren_Geo/Shutterstock.com; p. 23 Alex and Maria photo/Shutterstock.com; p. 25 https://commons.wikimedia.org/wiki/File:Erik_Weihenmayer_presenting_on_stage..jpg; p. 26 Torgado/Shutterstock.com; p. 27 SpeedKingz/Shutterstock.com; p. 29 Sangiao Photography/Shutterstock.com.

Cataloging-in-Publication Data

Names: Ratzer, Mary Boyd.
Title: Valuing differences / Mary Ratzer.
Description: Buffalo, NY : Rosen Young Adult, 2025. | Series: Spotlight on an equitable world | Includes glossary and index.
Identifiers: ISBN 9781499477368 (pbk.) | ISBN 9781499477283 (library bound) | ISBN 9781499477009 (ebook)
Subjects: LCSH: Cultural pluralism--Juvenile literature. | Difference (Psychology)--Juvenile literature. | Toleration--Juvenile literature.
Classification: LCC HM1271.R38 2025 | DDC 305.8--dc23

Manufactured in the United States of America

Some of the images in this book illustrate individuals who are models. The depictions do not imply actual situations or events.

CPSIA Compliance Information: Batch #CSRYA25. For further information contact Rosen Publishing at 1-800-237-9932.

CONTENTS

Chapter One

COULD YOU BE AN INFLUENCER?

As you grow up, you make decisions about your beliefs, values, and attitudes. These decisions shape the person you are and the person you'll become. They can lead to positive action. Can you encourage others to be aware of and accept people's differences? Could you learn more about the way others think, feel, and behave? If you have empathy, could you influence the attitudes of your friends and classmates? Could you encourage people to have good attitudes about differences?

Many young people value diversity and respect differences. Friendships often involve shared experiences and awareness. In a diverse country, many young people appreciate and are friends with people who are different from them. When you appreciate differences, you can better take part in community activities and friendships. You can counter prejudice with reality.

Many young people are ready to bring diverse people together. Studies prove that peers can influence others to think and behave in ways showing care and fairness. Friends influence each other in positive ways. People can resist negative peer influence. They can consider new perspectives. Teachers and other adult role models can help encourage open-mindedness and respect.

By working with your peers, you can build a positive school community that helps all students.

Chapter Two

CHECKING IN ON IDENTITY

People often develop more self-awareness and social awareness as they mature. Your identity may be a work in progress. Experiences, relationships, role models, and challenges shape the person you're becoming. Learning to value differences is a big step in developing your identity. Some young people, however, often only connect with people like themselves. A familiar group feels safe and comfortable. But the diverse world around you needs active citizens who welcome differences. You have the choice to use your values, goals, and strengths to take an active role in your community.

Look at the other students in your school. What are some things that you all share? How are you different from your peers?

Taking time to reflect on your own complex identity can give you insight into the identities of those around you. Consider the influences that have shaped your identity and your respect for those who are different from you. The statements below, taken from the National Social Justice Standards, can help you begin to explore and embrace the many differences you see in people in your world.

- **I know that I am a member of multiple groups in society.**
- **I can describe the group identities shared by my family.**
- **I understand that multiple identities create unique and complex people.**
- **I understand my connections with my family history and culture.**
- **I know that many identities make me who I am.**
- **I feel positive about my identities, but they do not make me better than anyone else.**
- **I know there are similarities and differences between cultures that I can describe.**
- **I show respect to people from all cultures and those who are different from me.**
- **I am curious about other cultures and family histories.**
- **I interact with people who are similar to and different from me.**

Chapter Three

VISIBLE AND INVISIBLE IDENTITIES

Your identity is a complex weave of characteristics that makes you unique. In some ways, you may be similar to your family, friends, and even strangers. Some characteristics of your identity are visible and can be observed by others. In some ways, however, you are different from even your closest relatives and your best friend. Some parts of your identity are personal and may not be apparent to others. When you build relationships, others may learn more about your invisible identity, and you may learn about theirs.

Someone can observe your abilities or your language. They might see your family structure and culture. Some visible aspects of your identity may include race, ethnicity, gender, and age. Some people may have biased perspectives and prejudices based on the visible identity of a person. However, visible cultural differences can also give you healthy confidence when you know who you are and are comfortable with it.

Invisible aspects of your identity are more personal. These may include the values you've formed over time, your religion, beliefs, and education. Only those who know you well may understand your talents and perspectives. Your life experiences will be invisible to many unless you share them. Your strengths will change over time and yet are an important part of your identity. Sometimes social pressure causes people to pretend to be something or value something just to fit in. That can have many troublesome consequences. It's important to be true to yourself.

The common phrase "You can't tell a book by it's cover" is true! You never know what a person is really like until you get to know them personally. Likewise, people won't know the real you unless you open up to them.

Chapter Four

BEING RESPECTFUL

Respect is learned and earned. Awareness of how to be respectful grows when you experience it from others. When you are respectful, you choose words and actions that build trust with others. In some ways, being respectful is like giving someone a gift of what you've learned about their rights and needs. When meeting someone new or someone different from you, your values and choices guide your respectful response to them. Being respectful even when it is difficult is a choice built into your character and identity.

Respecting yourself is a starting point for respecting others. Self-respect can give you confidence and the positive mindset needed to build respectful relationships. Expecting others to respect you without being respectful to yourself is an attitude that only leads to frustration.

Being respectful can result in a response that is equally respectful. Give respect, get respect.

Respect may also be a choice to have a positive attitude toward people of many types. It's good to be open minded and learn more about differences. The differences between groups of people may melt away after respectful interaction. Listening, caring, and learning about the character and qualities of a person can dissolve stereotypes and disrespect. Have you gotten to know someone who seemed different from you but turned out to have many qualities you value in a friend?

Think about this as you engage with family, friends, classmates, and teachers. Think about what you could contribute to your community when you choose respect.

Chapter Five

ASK ME ABOUT MY CULTURE!

Culture includes the customs, traditions, and activities of a group of people. As the United States becomes even more diverse, interest in cultures can serve as a bridge between different people. Curiosity and a willingness to listen in good faith can lead to open conversations about culture. It's important, however, to be sure you don't put all the work of education on the other person—and that you understand that not everyone can take part in all aspects of other cultures.

Culture is meaningful for many people. In many neighborhoods, communities, and schools, cultural celebrations may bring people together with enthusiasm. This can be a chance to support small businesses owned by people of that culture, with chances to learn about food, arts, music, books, and more. Community groups may plan special cultural events such as festivals, markets, music or dance performances, or open houses. These shared experiences can open the door to building relationships and partnerships.

A polite greeting or a question can start a conversation about cultures. Students may wish to share information about theirs. For example, perhaps a group including you and your fellow students would want to band together and present a multicultural panel to visit assemblies and classes across a large school district. Other students could ask you about their culture and what you love about it, including arts, languages, customs, daily life, or religion. However, even shorter interactions can encourage sharing about backgrounds, ethnicity, and culture.

All cultures have interesting and surprising aspects that can be fun and educational to share with others. What would you tell others about your culture?

Chapter Six

FERTILE GROUND AND DIVERSE COMMUNITIES

Fertile soil provides a place for diverse seeds to grow. In a similar way, diverse communities are places where many cultures can flourish. Differences based on many things can help communities thrive. They're more likely to have a deep and varied connection to arts, music, language, and stories. These cultural assets are valuable, and they can add energy to the communities that embrace them.

A community mural project can provide community members with a chance to work together and share important aspects of their cultures.

Diverse communities throughout the United States may be home to arts organizations, resident artists, wide-ranging musical talent, amazing food, and other aspects of their many cultures. These things may draw in people from outside the community and boost the local economy. Diverse communities may have a high level of community engagement and decreasing poverty rates. The benefits of a diverse community can include greater social connections and reduced barriers based on class and ethnicity. Diversity can bring new life to communities.

We need diversity to be creative and healthy, and you might see how that works in the world around you. Does a marching band celebrate the identity of a community and school? Can a street mural show off local creative talent and reflect the community? Can local performers showcase the diverse music of their community? Absolutely.

Chapter Seven

HAWAII, FIRE, AND 'OHANA

In August 2023, wildfires swept over a town called Lahaina and other areas on the Hawaiian island of Maui. Whipped up by high winds and dry conditions, the fire spread with deadly speed. Many people lost everything they owned, and others lost their lives. Thousands needed relief, rescue, shelter, medical care, water, food, and other necessities. As the rest of the United States watched this disaster and its aftermath unfold, more people learned about the idea of *'ohana*.

'Ohana means family. The idea has roots in ancient Hawaiian culture and that of other Polynesian cultures. It's broader than just the idea of parents and their children and more than blood connections. It includes the respectful responsibility for the well-being of the community. In this case, "family" includes everyone in Lahaina.

This photograph shows the extent of the destruction in Lahaina after the wildfires of August 2023.

You might be familiar with the concept of ʻohana from the Disney movie *Lilo and Stitch*. This movie emphasizes the close bond between two characters from different planets! Talk about sharing different cultures!

Many people know that ʻohana means nobody gets left behind or forgotten. It goes beyond that as well. Everyone has what they need to live a good life. Relationships go beyond blood and include the community as a whole. People take care of each other and step up to help when they can. A Hawaii state fund for the families of those killed in the wildfire has been named the One ʻOhana Fund.

ʻOhana is an important part of Hawaiian culture. In other cultures as well, members of a community are often connected. The people in your biological family, your school or work family, social groups to which you belong, neighbors, and friends provide support in different areas of your life. Social groups try to work together to support community members. Valuing each person as a part of an extended family can lead to care and connections. This idea goes beyond taking care of physical needs. Caring for emotional needs is also important. Community ties can help when people face challenging times.

Chapter Eight

BARBIE DOLLS AND REAL-WORLD DIFFERENCES

If you haven't played with Barbie dolls yourself, you probably knew someone who did or does. In some ways, Barbie has changed a bit from the always blonde, tall, slim doll of the 1960s and 1970s. Mattel, the company that manufactures Barbie, decided to bring more aspects and versions of the doll into the modern world. Mattel listened to those with differences, and many more people can now see themselves reflected in the dolls.

Consumers sent a clear message that the old image of Barbie had to change. The changes were made with input and careful guidance from many people, and more Barbies now reflect real people a little more. Their appearance mirrors the differences that are a part of real life. Barbies represent more body types and ethnicities. They come in more shapes and sizes. Some Barbies use a wheelchair, hearing aids, or prosthetic limbs. Recently, the National Down Syndrome Society helped create one of the dolls. A young advocate with Down syndrome, Kayla McKeon, worked so people like her could see themselves in a famous toy.

A push toward diversity (and public demand) propelled the changes at Mattel. It's important that people not only see themselves in different sorts of toys, it's also important that others, especially kids, can see and play with toys that reflect real-world people and differences.

Matel now offers several Barbies that come with wheelchairs. They also come with other accessories, including a wheelchair ramp and fashionable clothing.

Chapter Nine

SOCIAL MEDIA GROUPS AND DIFFERENCES

Experiences with social media can get a lot of attention. Recent surveys show some insights into how differences between people play out on social media. In some cases, researchers went directly to teens and middle schoolers to look closely at social media.

In 2022, the Pew Research Center conducted a survey of U.S. teens ages 13 to 17. The results showed that eight in ten teens feel that social media makes them more in touch with their friends. Over seven in ten reported that social media lets them share their creativity. Almost as many confirm that they use social media platforms to show support for others dealing with problems. In general, many teens said they feel more accepted on social media platforms.

Teens agreed that social media helped them learn about people who are different from them. Black or Hispanic teens were more likely than white teens to say what they see on social media makes them feel a lot of support and a lot more accepted. This has been a trend for a number of years. Three out of four teens who participated say that the online groups introduced them to new people and connected them with others.

About six in ten teens have at least one close friend online or in person of a different racial or ethnic background or a different gender. Teen girls of color using TikTok said they found positive outlets for expression, connections, and social activism.

Social media platforms allow us to connect with people all over the world. Think of all the unique people there are to meet and share ideas with!

Chapter Ten

VALUING DIFFERENCES IN YOUR BRAIN

Rosie King was 10 years old when she first read a book about autism. She realized that she was someone whose brain works in a different way. The same year, she illustrated a book her mother published. Rosie has a creative spark, an energetic mind, and a lot of curiosity. As a teenager, she began to speak more about celebrating her differences. In 2014, she did a talk about "How Autism Freed Me to Be Myself," which now has more than 800,000 views on YouTube. Rosie shares the many positives that come with how her brain works due to autism.

Rosie still works as an activist. She sees the pull to be normal as strong but very limiting. She knows that it can be a challenge to be a friend to someone who is different. Trying to fit into the "tiny box

Autism (short for autism spectrum disorder) can be many things. Not everyone with it has the same symptoms, or signs.

of normal," she says, many kids hide their differences. Rosie is one of many people working to change the perspective that differences like hers are negative. She asks why people are "pouring their brilliant, individual light into a mold?"

Doctors identify a number of strengths connected to differences in the brain. These skills can include creativity, recognizing patterns, analyzing, focusing, and remembering things. Do your teachers encourage you to identify and celebrate differences? Seeing these differences as disabilities to be feared leaves out a lot of possibilities. Maybe you or your friends have differences like this. Remember that they should be celebrated! Speaking up can show people different ways of thinking.

Chapter Eleven

THE WONDER OF DIFFERENCES

Evelyn Glennie is a musician, composer, and solo performer. Born in Scotland, she has been deaf since age 12. Her talent with instruments, especially drums, has won her many awards and honors. She performed in the Olympics opening ceremony in 2012 and has teamed up with many other musical greats. She often plays barefoot during live performances to better feel the music and has trained herself to feel music in different parts of her body. Her speech, "How to Truly Listen," has been viewed more than 6 million times on YouTube.

Erik Weihenmayer was about 14 years old when he fully lost his sight. But he wouldn't let blindness limit his possibilities. As a teen, he began rock climbing, using his hands and feet to feel for holds. As a middle school teacher and coach, Erik climbed the highest peak in North America, Denali in Alaska. From there, he joined only 150 others in the world who had climbed the seven highest mountains on the planet. This included Mount Everest, the world's tallest peak. His attitude got him to the top of the world.

The Special Olympics can change the lives of people with intellectual disabilities. Through the power of sports, athletes can discover and show off their strengths and abilities. The Invictus Games bring together athletes, some still in the military and some veterans, who've been injured or have other differences. These athletes show the world their skills and talents along with their mental strength and determination. All have differences that are part of them but do not define who they are.

Erik Weihenmayer is also a motivational speaker. He talks about his life experiences and reaching new heights despite his disability, inspiring others to do the same.

Chapter Twelve

FITTING IN, STANDING OUT

Many people are motivated to fit in and be "normal," whatever they consider normal to be. This is true for adults, kids, and people your age. Your classmates may influence your attitudes and actions about differences in other people. Many times, young people who are different from others can be bullied for not conforming or matching the others around them. Still, people can be proud of their self-defined identity and ignore peer pressure to fit in. Others appreciate and take opportunities to engage with others who are different. Everyone can grow in their understanding of and appreciation for differences.

It can be hard to go against your peers. But valuing the differences you see in others—or yourself—can sometimes require you to disagree with those close to you.

Often, people with any sort of differences may be targeted and exposed to criticism, negative attitudes, isolation, or worse. You may notice groups who hold similar beliefs, attitudes, and perspectives on differences. They may resist interacting with others outside their group. However, others will mature and learn to value differences. Some people, focused more on themselves, may never do so!

If you're concerned about how you, your friends, or others are treated because of differences, you should act. When others are excluded or mistreated, you can refuse to be a part of these actions. You can use your voice to speak out for yourself and others. You can celebrate your own differences, be an ally to other people, or both!

Chapter Thirteen

CHECKING IN ON BIAS

People your age can be subject to stereotypes and biased attitudes just because of that age. One common stereotype applied to people in the middle grades and high school is that you're impulsive, take risks, make poor decisions, and rebel. Do you think those things are true? People your age are getting ready to be more independent, and you're probably ready to take risks in a move positive way. You might want to take part in and look at new experiences, hobbies, interests, and identities.

Other stereotypes say that teens are focused on themselves, don't like adults, and need adult decision-makers to guide their actions. Like all stereotypes, these are largely untrue! Many young people are growing more self-aware, and this can be a force for social awareness and positive action. You can benefit greatly from relationships with adults beyond your parents, such as coaches, teachers, and other mentors. Your own personal agency can be a powerful outlet for your talents and strengths.

Bias needs certain conditions to survive. It needs a willingness to accept opinions without testing their truth. It needs unquestioning comfort with unfair attitudes. Bias doesn't thrive when relationships and experiences are the basis for attitudes. It rarely survives when you value fairness above going along with what others think. Questioning attitudes or beliefs can be a start to curbing bias. Reflecting on the reasons for a point of view can give you a chance to reconsider a perspective with honesty.

Becoming more self-aware means finding a style you like. But it also means respecting the styles of others.

Chapter Fourteen

DOING YOUR PART

An inclusive community is a safe place where responsible citizens work together to actively be a part of positive change. What is your role as a part of a community and an active citizen? How can you do your part? Consider the following questions as you prepare to become part of a community that truly values differences.

- **Do you see yourself as an active part of a community? In what way?**
- **Do you respect and appreciate differences and learn about the diverse cultures and people in your community?**
- **Do you work to understand the similarities and differences you see in your community?**
- **Do you communicate and engage with others to build new relationships?**
- **Do you understand how your actions affect others?**
- **Are you concerned about how people are treated, and do you empathize with those who are treated unfairly because of their identity?**
- **Do you stand up for yourself and others when bias or unfairness happens?**
- **Do you work to understand the perspectives of others?**
- **Do you speak up and act for equity and fairness when you recognize unfairness in your community?**
- **Do you work with friends, family, and community members to set goals and find solutions for problems?**

By contemplating these questions and forming thoughtful answers, you can learn more about yourself, your community, and the many people who help make it a great place to live. By valuing the differences you see around you, you directly contribute to the process of creating an equitable world.

GLOSSARY

autism: A disorder characterized especially by problems in interacting and communicating with other people and by doing some activities over and over again.

bias: To have an unfair preference or dislike of something.

criticism: The act of judging something, especially finding fault.

determination: A firm or fixed intension about a course of action.

Down syndrome: A genetic condition characterized by developmental delays, distinctive physical traits, and by the presence of three chromosomes numbered 21 in human beings.

empathy: Being aware of and sharing another person's feelings, experiences, and emotions.

enthusiasm: A strong excitement and active interest.

inclusive: Inviting to all people.

isolation: Being set apart from others; being alone.

perspective: Point of view.

prejudice: Unfriendly feelings directed against an individual, a group, or a race.

prosthetic: Having to do with an artificial device to replace or augment a missing or impaired part of the body.

stereotype: An unfair and often untrue belief about someone or a group of people.

INDEX